Grandmother's Precious Baby

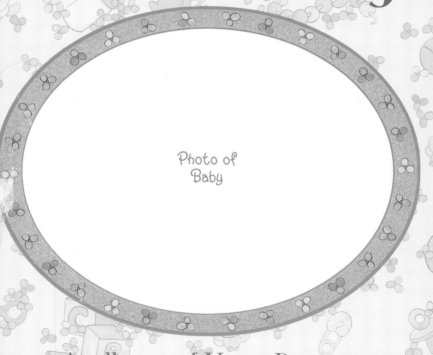

Photo of
Baby

A collection of Verses, Prayers,
and Thoughts of Love from a
Grandmother's Heart

Every good gift and every perfect gift is from above, and comes down from the Father of lights.

James 1:17

One look tells the whole story. Peering through a mass of tightly bound hospital blankets, this new little bundle of joy embraces the world with eyes like Grandpa. A chin like yours. And dimples that flash in a near, newborn smile — the same way your own baby's did when you first held that precious gift from God not so long ago. The circle of love has begun again — and you, dear Grandmother, complete this band of support.

Grandmother's Precious Baby helps you begin to record on page the special feelings and memories you hold most dear to your heart. The gentle innocence of **Precious Moments**® portraits alongside beautiful Scripture promises paint a rainbow of hope for your beloved grandchild. It also provides a place for you to record prayers, hopes, and pictures as a beautiful reminder of this blessed beginning and a tangible token of your faith and love.

Let Me Tell You About My New Angel!

_____
Name

Born _____
Date and Time

Hospital _____
City, State

Weight _____ Length _____

Our Family Tree

_____   _____
Mother   Father

_____   _____
Grandmother   Grandmother

_____   _____
Grandfather   Grandfather

_____   _____   _____   _____
Great-   Great-   Great-   Great-
Grandmother   Grandmother   Grandmother   Grandmother

_____   _____   _____   _____
Great-   Great-   Great-   Great-
Grandfather   Grandfather   Grandfather   Grandfather

Brothers and Sisters

_____

_____

_____

_____

_____

Special Memories...

While Mommy was expecting _____

_____

_____

My arrival day _____

_____

_____

Welcome home, Precious! _____

_____

_____

_____

_____

Special Gifts from Those Who Love Me

_____

_____

_____

Special Church Occasion

On_____ At _____.
Date Time

_____
Baby's Name

Was_____
Ceremony Performed

By_____ At _____.
Church Official Where

_____   _____
Godmother   Godfather

_____   _____
Witness   Witness

Photo

My Angel

"Before I formed you in the womb I knew you; before you were born I sanctified you."

Jeremiah 1:5

We have a spiritual heritage that goes beyond generations. Our roots in Christ run back before time, when the Creator of the universe conceived us, and put into motion His plan to bring forth His children in His perfect time. Now your grandchild's debut has arrived, and it is your privilege to pass on the Father's legacy of love.

The following scriptures read as love letters from Father to child. Read them to your grandchildren and remind them of their special place in God's heart. Realize the promises are as true for you as for this tiny miracle in your arms. And rejoice that the same God who saw you and your family before time began will keep watch over you still, and safely lead you through life as you lean on His Word.

Behold, children are a
heritage from the LORD,
The fruit of the womb
is a reward.
Like arrows in the hand
of a warrior,
So are the children
of one's youth.
Happy is the [one] who has
his quiver full of them.

Psalm 127:3–5

For He shall
give His angels
charge over you,
To keep you
in all your ways.

Psalm 91:11

For I know
the thoughts that
I think toward you,
says the LORD,
thoughts of peace
and not of evil,
to give you a future
and a hope.

Jeremiah 29:11

For you are our glory and joy.

1 Thessalonians 2:20

Jesus said,
"Let the little
children come to Me,
and do not forbid
them; for of such
is the kingdom
of heaven."

Matthew 19:14

Behold what
manner of love
the Father has
bestowed on us,
that we should be
called children
of God!

1 John 3:1

The father of
the righteous will
greatly rejoice,
And he who
begets a wise
child will delight
in him.

Proverbs 23:24

May the LORD
give you increase more
and more,
You and your children.
May you be blessed
by the LORD,
Who made heaven
and earth.

Psalm 115:14–15

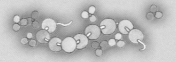

May He grant
you according to
your heart's
desire,
And fulfill
all your purpose.

Psalm 20:4

I will both
lie down in peace,
and sleep;
For you alone,
O LORD,
make me dwell
in safety.

Psalm 4:8

Train up a child
in the way he
should go,
And when he
is old he will not
depart from it.

Proverbs 22:6

"The LORD bless you
and keep you;
The LORD make His
face shine upon you,
And be gracious
to you;
The LORD lift up His
countenance upon you,
And give you peace."

Numbers 6:24-26

"Before I formed
you in the womb
I knew you;
Before
you were born
I sanctified you."

Jeremiah 1:5

Children's children
are the crown
of old men,
And the glory
of children
is their father.

Proverbs 17:6

I have no greater joy than to hear that my children walk in truth.

3 John 4

And now abide
faith, hope, love,
these three;
but the greatest
of these is love.

1 Corinthians 13:13

"As the Father loved Me, I also have loved you; abide in My love."

John 15:9

"The LORD your God
in your midst,
The Mighty One,
will save;
He will rejoice
over you with gladness,
He will quiet you
with His love,
He will rejoice
over you with singing."

Zephaniah 3:17

A Special Prayer
for My Angel...

My _____

_____

_____

_____

_____

_____

_____

_____

_____

_____

_____

_____

_____

_____